BEGINN

STARTING OUT MY CHRISTIAN LIFE

7 Obstacles Along the Way

SERENDIPITY HOUSE / BOX 1012 / LITTLETON, CO 80160 / TOLL FREE 1-800-525-9563
96 97 98 99 / **YTH series•CHG** / 6 5 4 3 2 1

Contents: 7 Sessions

BEFORE ... DURING ... AFTER

Progress Report

We will check to see where you are three times during this course—at the end of the ...

- First session
- Fourth session
- Seventh session

If you had a complete physical, mental, relational and spiritual check-up at the Mayo Clinic by doctors in these fields, what would they conclude about you? Record your pulse in each of these areas by putting a dot on the line below to indicate how you see yourself—1 being POOR and 10 being EXCELLENT health.

Physically: I am feeling good physically. I stay in shape by exercising regularly and eating right. I sleep well and enjoy life. Physically, I am ...

Poor ————————————————— Excellent

    1 2 3 4 5 6 (7) 8 9 10

Mentally: I am feeling good about myself. I build myself up. I have some God-given abilities. I am aware of my strengths. I like who I am. Mentally, I am ...

Poor ————————————————— Excellent

    1 2 3 4 5 6 (7) 8 9 10

Relationally: I am feeling good about sharing myself with others. I make friends well. I deal with conflict. I reach out, care and forgive. Relationally, I am ...

Poor ————————————————— Excellent

    1 2 3 4 5 (6) 7 8 9 10

Spiritually: I am feeling good about my relationship with God. I am getting my spiritual life together, putting God first. Spiritually, I am ...

Poor ————————————————— Excellent

    1 2 3 4 5 (6) 7 8 9 10

Love the Lord your God with all your heart and with all your soul and with all your mind and with all your strength. Love your neighbor as yourself.

Mark 12:30–31

3

LEADER:
Before you start, read A Word to the Youth Leaders, on page 46.

SESSION 1
Rookie Year

CROWD BREAKER

LEADER:
Pass out books. Explain teamwork principle. Explain diagrams on page 46 and theory behind 2's, 4's and 8's. Read Introduction out loud and break into teams of 8—preferably with a leader assigned to each team.

See *Coach's Book.*

Introduction: Welcome to this course on getting a good start in the Christian life. Your youth leader has probably explained how this program works and the importance of teamwork. In each session you will do a series of exercises—starting out with groups of 2, then moving into groups of 4, and finally groups of 8. The reason for this is to give you a chance to participate in the size of group that is most suitable for what you are doing.

Groups of 2 / 15 minutes

CONVERSATION STARTER

LEADER:
Have the group pair off in 2's for the Conservation Starter. (If you have less than six youth, you may want to stay together for the entire meeting.) Call time after 15 minutes and move to Bible Study.

How's It Going? Now, to get started, pair off with one other person from your team and give a quick picture of yourself. What kind of day did you have today? What kind of year are you having? Mark where you fit on each of the lines below which best describes your day or your year. Then share what you marked with your partner. If you have time left over, talk about why you answered like you did.

Sunny _____ Stormy

I felt like royalty _____ I felt like a gym shoe

Super Model_____Bad hair day

Wonder Dog _____Fire Hydrant

Tazmanian Devil_____Sleep the Dwarf

Mother Teresa _____Madonna

Statue _____Pigeon

Energizer Bunny _____Dead Battery

Barefoot in the Park _____*Nightmare on Elm Street*

Groups of 4 / 15–30 minutes

The First "Rookies." The Bible study time in this session is a little different from the usual Bible study because the purpose of the course is different. The purpose of this course is to get to know each other and to become a team.

LEADER:
Put two groups of 2 together to make groups of 4. Rearrange chairs. Read Introduction and Scripture aloud. Save 30 minutes for the last part—Caring Time.

For this session, the Bible story is about four people whom Jesus invited to be on his team. Your youth leader may want to explain the expression "Lamb of God" that John the Baptist used to describe Jesus Christ.

The Bible study has two parts: (1) **Looking Into the Story**— about the story in the Bible, and (2) **My Own Story**—about your own experience. There is a discussion questionnaire with multiple-choice options for you to choose. There are no right or wrong answers ... so you can feel free to share your opinion. We recommend that you divide into groups of 4 for this Bible study—so that everyone can participate in the discussion and finish in 30 minutes. Be sure to save the last 30 minutes at the close to decide on your goals, expectations and ground rules for this course.

Now, listen to the Bible story. Then, quickly move into groups of 4 and discuss the questionnaire.

35The next day John was there again with two of his disciples. 36When he saw Jesus passing by, he said, "Look, the Lamb of God!"

37When the two disciples heard him say this, they followed Jesus. 38Turning around, Jesus saw them following and asked, "What do you want?"

They said, "Rabbi" (which means Teacher), "where are you staying?"

39"Come," he replied, "and you will see."

So they went and saw where he was staying, and spent that day with him. It was about the tenth hour.

40Andrew, Simon Peter's brother, was one of the two who heard what John had said and who had followed Jesus. 41The first thing Andrew did was to find his brother Simon and tell him, "We have found the Messiah" (that is, the Christ). 42And he brought him to Jesus.

Jesus looked at him and said, "You are Simon son of John. You will be called Cephas" (which, when translated, is Peter).

43The next day Jesus decided to leave for Galilee. Finding Philip, he said to him, "Follow me."

44Philip, like Andrew and Peter, was from the town of Bethsaida. 45Philip found Nathanael and told him, "We have found the one Moses wrote about in the Law, and about whom the prophets also wrote—Jesus of Nazareth, the son of Joseph."

46"Nazareth! Can anything good come from there?" Nathanael asked.

"Come and see," said Philip.

47When Jesus saw Nathanael approaching, he said of him, "Here is a true Israelite, in whom there is nothing false."

48"How do you know me?" Nathanael asked.

Jesus answered, "I saw you while you were still under the fig tree before Philip called you."

⁴⁹Then Nathanael declared, "Rabbi, you are the Son of God; you are the King of Israel."

⁵⁰Jesus said, "You believe because I told you I saw you under the fig tree. You shall see greater things than that." ⁵¹He then added, "I tell you the truth, you shall see heaven open, and the angels of God ascending and descending on the Son of Man."

John 1:35–51

Looking Into the Story: In groups of 4, let one person answer question #1, the next person answer question #2, etc. around your group. There are no right or wrong answers, so feel free to express your opinion.

1. If you were a Hollywood film director and you wanted to make a film about the life of Jesus Christ, who would you want to play the part of Jesus?
   - ☑ Kevin Costner
   - ❏ Emilio Estaves
   - ❏ Denzel Washington
   - ❏ Michael Douglas
   - ❏ other:_____

2. What is the most obvious indication that the two disciples in the first part of the story were "rookies" spiritually?
   - ❏ They were following around the "star," gawking at him.
   - ❏ They abruptly switched from following John to following Jesus.
   - ❏ They did not even know what they were looking for when Jesus asked.
   - ☑ They had a rookie's enthusiasm—spending all day learning from their "coach," then telling everyone else about him.

3. Jesus asked the two disciples, "What do you want?" but they never really answered his question. What do *you* think they really wanted?
   - ❏ friendship—someone to care for and accept them
   - ❏ entertainment—someone to do miracles and amuse them
   - ☑ life meaning—someone to show them what life was about
   - ❏ healing—someone to help them get over emotional wounds

4. Jesus gave Simon a nickname (both Cephas and Peter mean *rock*). What does that say about Simon?
   - ❏ that he was strong and very courageous
   - ❏ that he had the potential of being strong
   - ❏ that he was not really strong, but would learn to be strong
   - ☑ that God was going to completely change his personality

5. Nathanael made a comment about Nazareth, Jesus' hometown (v. 46). What does it mean?
   a. Nazareth had a bad reputation.
   b. Nazareth was a low-class town.
   c. Nazareth never produced a state championship in anything.

6. What was Jesus' invitation to all of these guys?
   ☑ Commit your life to me.
   ☐ Give me a test drive.
   ☐ Don't trust what others have said about me.
   ☐ The Christian life is not for spectators.

My Own Story: Note how the instructions are going to change for the second half of the Bible study. Take question #1 and let everyone in the group share their answer. Then, take question #2 and go around again, etc. through the questions. Be sure to save the last 30 minutes in this session to get back together and make some very important decisions about this course.

1. Do you have a nickname? What is it?

2. If you had to give yourself a nickname for your spiritual life right now, what would it be?

☐ rock	☐ second stringer
☐ rocky	☐ yo-yo
☐ rookie	☐ die-hard
☐ veteran	☑ fence-rider
☐ bench warmer	☐ other:_____

3. If Jesus asked you right now, "What do you want?" how would you respond? Rank the following responses from "1" (what you want the most) to "4" (what you want the least):

   _2_ friendship—someone to care for and accept me
   _1_ entertainment—someone to keep me from being bored
   _3_ life meaning—someone to show me what life is about
   _4_ healing—someone to help me get over some painful things

4. How would you describe your own status as a Christian?
   ☐ I'm a rookie—just learning what I'm really looking for.
   ☐ I'm in my sophomore season—I still have much to learn.
   ☐ I'm a seasoned veteran—I feel solid in my faith.
   ☐ I haven't made it out of the minors yet!
   ☑ I'm playing another game entirely!

Groups of 8 / 30 minutes

 Team Sign-Up. Now is the time to decide what you want to get out of this course. For yourself. For your team. And for you to agree on the ground rules for teamwork. Follow these four steps.

Step 1: Check-In. Turn to page 3 and let everyone on your team explain where they are right now in these areas of their life. (You will have a chance to retake this test at the close of the course to see where you have grown.)

Step 2: Expectations. Give everyone a chance to share the top two things they would like to get out of this course, using the list below:

❏ to have fun
❏ to get closer as a youth group
❏ to hang out with my friends
❏ to reach out to other kids at school
❏ to talk about the real stuff in my life

❏ to get to know the Bible
❏ to grow in my faith
❏ other:_____

Step 3: Ground Rules. What are a couple of things on the list below that you would like to include in the ground rules for being in this course? See if you can agree on these.

❏ ATTENDANCE: I will be at all six remaining sessions.

❏ OPENNESS: I will share my thoughts and feelings openly each week.

❏ CONFIDENTIALITY: I will keep anything that is said at the meetings in confidence.

❏ PRAYER: I will pray for the others on my team.

❏ REACH OUT: I will invite others to join our group.

❏ SERVICE: I would like to see our team commit to a mission project at the close of this course.

❏ CELEBRATION: I would like to see us end this course together with a party or retreat.

❏ ACCOUNTABILITY: I would like to see us report in each week on our spiritual walk with Christ.

Step 4: Prayer Partner. Within your team, choose one or two others to conclude this meeting, and every meeting for the next six sessions, with a time of prayer. Before you pray, share how you are feeling, and how you want your prayer partner to pray for you this week. Then, call during the week to ask, "How's it going?"

SESSION 2
Playing Field

CROWD BREAKER

See *Coach's Book.*

Groups of 2 / 15 minutes

CONVERSATION STARTER

LEADER:
Recap the last session. Repeat the teamwork principles. Ask teams of 8 to divide into groups of 2—not the same person as last session.

Scavenger Hunt. In the last session, you decided to "go for it" and committed yourself to be a support group.

In this session, you are going to check out your spiritual growth. To get started, get together with one other person from your team (not the same person as last week) and work on this exercise together. If you have a wallet or purse, use the first set of questions below. If you do not have your wallet or purse with you, use the second set of questions below. This is like a scavenger hunt. You get two minutes in silence to go through your possessions or think about your answers. Then, you break the silence and "show and tell" to your partner what you have found. For instance, "The thing I have had for the longest time in my wallet is this picture of me when I was a baby."

Now, get together with your partner and take two minutes in silence to find the items on this scavenger hunt.

WALLET OR PURSE LIST OF ITEMS (Finish the sentence)

1. The thing I have had for the LONGEST TIME is ...
2. The thing that has SENTIMENTAL VALUE is ...
3. The thing that reminds me of a FUN TIME is ...
4. The thing that causes me a lot of CONCERN is ...
5. The thing that means a lot to me because of the PERSON that gave it to me is ...

IF YOU DON'T HAVE YOUR WALLET OR PURSE (Finish the sentence)

1. The most EXPENSIVE thing I am wearing is ...
2. The CHEAPEST thing I am wearing is ...
3. The one thing that I CARRY with me all the time is ...
4. The thing I wear that has SENTIMENTAL VALUE is ...
5. The thing that means a lot to me because of the PERSON who gave it to me is ...

Groups of 4 / 15–30 minutes

Bloom Where You Are Planted. Stop the camera. If a soil inspector came today to inspect the soils in your life, what would they find?

LEADER

Combine two groups of 2 to make groups of 4. Read Introduction and Scripture. Call time 20 minutes before closing time.

Jesus used this parable to explain why some people show the results of a healthy, balanced spiritual life, and some do not. In this session, you will have a chance to measure your output and see if you can improve it. Listen to the Bible story. Then, move into groups of 4 and discuss the questionnaire: (1) **Looking Into the Story**—about the Bible story, and (2) **My Own Story**—about your own experience.

Be sure to save the last 20 minutes at the close of this session for the Caring Time. Now, listen to the Bible story. Then, move into groups of 4 to share your responses.

⁴While a large crowd was gathering and people were coming to Jesus from town after town, he told this parable: ⁵"A farmer went out to sow his seed. As he was scattering the seed, some fell along the path; it was trampled on, and the birds of the air ate it up. ⁶Some fell on rock, and when it came up, the plants withered because they had no moisture. ⁷Other seed fell among thorns, which grew up with it and choked the plants. ⁸Still other seed fell on good soil. It came up and yielded a crop, a hundred times more than was sown."

When he said this, he called out, "He who has ears to hear, let him hear." ...

¹¹"This is the meaning of the parable: The seed is the word of God. ¹²Those along the path are the ones who hear, and then the devil comes and takes away the word from their hearts, so that they may not believe and be saved. ¹³Those on the rock are the ones who receive the word with joy when they hear it, but they have no root. They believe for a while, but in the time of testing they fall away. ¹⁴The seed that fell among thorns stands for those who hear, but as they go on their way they are choked by life's worries, riches and pleasures, and they do not mature. ¹⁵But the seed on good soil stands for those with a noble and good heart, who hear the word, retain it, and by persevering produce a crop.

Luke 8:4–8,11–15

Looking Into the Story: In groups of 4, let one person answer question #1, the next person answer question #2, etc. around the group.

1.   As you listened to the description of the four soils in the Scripture, what was your first impression?
     ❐ Oh no, this is going to be a boring Bible study.
     ☒ I wonder which soil I am.
     ❐ What is Jesus trying to say?
     ❐ Sounds like some state fair 4-H lecture.

2. Why did Jesus say, "He who has ears to hear, let him hear"?
   - ☐ The message he gave was not "closed-captioned for the hearing impaired."
   - ☐ People were throwing spit wads at each other in the back row.
   - ☑ Some people were not ready to hear what he was saying.
   - ☐ His message was simple enough for anyone who was really listening.

3. If Jesus were trying to get across the same message today, using images more familiar to you, what might he say?
   - ☐ Keep hitting the ball hard—yeah, some get caught, but eventually some will fall for hits.
   - ☑ No matter how good the teacher is, some students will get it, and some students won't.
   - ☐ Bloom where you are planted—but don't neglect to tend the soil!
   - ☐ Keep putting in those job applications—you will get a lot of rejections, but it only takes one "yes"!

4. Try to match what is said about the four soils in the parable with the four kids listed below and on the next page:

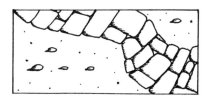 

STEVE is the first one to volunteer for anything. He's also the first one to drop out when the going gets rough. He makes a lot of promises but only lives up to the ones that are easy to keep. Compared to the four soils in this parable, Steve is like the:

CRAIG is a great guy. He's always the life of the party and always on the move. He never slows down to think about anything serious. He gets bored easily and takes a so-so attitude toward anything that gets "heavy." Craig is like the:

CARA is the kind of girl you can really depend on to get the job done. She works hard for the things that are important to her. Even if things are hard, she hangs in there. Cara will always give it her best shot. She is like the:

SHELLY is into enjoying life to its fullest. She wants to be seen with the cutest guys, wear the best clothes, and belong to the most popular groups. She changes her views to fit the group she's with at the time. She would never risk doing anything that might be considered unpopular. When things don't go her way, she pouts or gets mad. Shelly is like the:

My Own Story: Note the shift in the way to discuss the second half of the questionnaire. Take question #1 and let everyone share their answer. Then, take question #2 and go around again. Be sure to save the last 20 minutes in the session for the Caring Time.

1. What are the "thorns" and "rocks" in your life which tend to choke out your spiritual growth? (Choose as many as apply.)
    - ❐ peer pressure
    - ❐ material possessions
    - ❐ influence of TV/movies/music
    - ❐ sexual temptations
    - ❐ lack of commitment/discipline
    - ❐ parties/alcohol/drugs
    - ❐ a "rocky" home life
    - ☑ worry about my future
    - ❐ suffering that makes it hard to believe in a good God

2. What do you have in your life that gives "depth to your soil" and nurtures your growth? (Choose as many as apply, and put a star by the one that is most important to you.)
    - ❐ Christian parents
    - ❐ this group
    - ❐ other Christian relatives
    - ❐ my private devotions
    - ❐ Christian friends
    - ❐ Christian music
    - ❐ regular worship
    - ❐ some books I've read
    - ❐ Sunday School
    - ❐ other: _School_

3. When in the last couple of years did the ground seem particularly "thorny" or "rocky" so that you felt your faith was threatened? What helped you through that time?

    A friend.

4. What percentage of time do you spend each day doing each of the following?
    - _50_ % unnecessary (wasted)
    - _20_ % necessary but unexciting (boring)
    - _20_ % exciting but not lasting (unproductive)
    - _10_ % exciting and lasting (productive)

5. What does the following Scripture say about your life right now?

    [7]Do not be deceived: God cannot be mocked. A man reaps what he sows. [8]The one who sows to please his sinful nature, from that nature will reap destruction; the one who sows to please the Spirit, from the Spirit will reap eternal life.

    Galatians 6:7–8

    What I do to others will happen to me

Groups of 8 / 15–20 minutes

 Team Check-In: How's It Going? After two sessions in this program, stop the camera and evaluate what you think about the program ... and what you would like to change. Regather with your team and go over the questions together. Be sure to save the last few minutes to be with your prayer partner (Step 3).

LEADER: Bring teams back together for Step 1 and 2. Then, Step 3 with prayer partners for this course.

Step 1: Check Your Pulse. What do you appreciate most about this course? Go around and let everyone share one or two things.

___ fun times
___ studying the Bible
___ close relationships
___ feeling like I belong
___ sharing our problems
___ praying for each other
___ reaching out to others
___ other:_____

Step 2: I Wish. If you could have one wish for this program, what would it be? Finish the sentence, "I wish we could have ..."

___ more sharing about each other
___ more time for Bible Study
___ more fun
___ more reaching out
___ more special events
___ less joking around
___ less gossip
___ less study
___ other:_____

Step 3: Prayer Partner. Get together with the prayer partner you started with last week, and describe the last seven days in your life as a weather report. Then, close in prayer for each other. Finish the sentence, "This past week has been ..."

❏ blue sky, bright sunshine all week long—NO PROBLEMS
❏ partly cloudy most of the week—A FEW PROBLEMS
❏ severe storms all week long
❏ mixed—some days sunny, some days cloudy
❏ warming trend—getting better
❏ tornado/hurricane—DISASTERS!
❏ other:_____

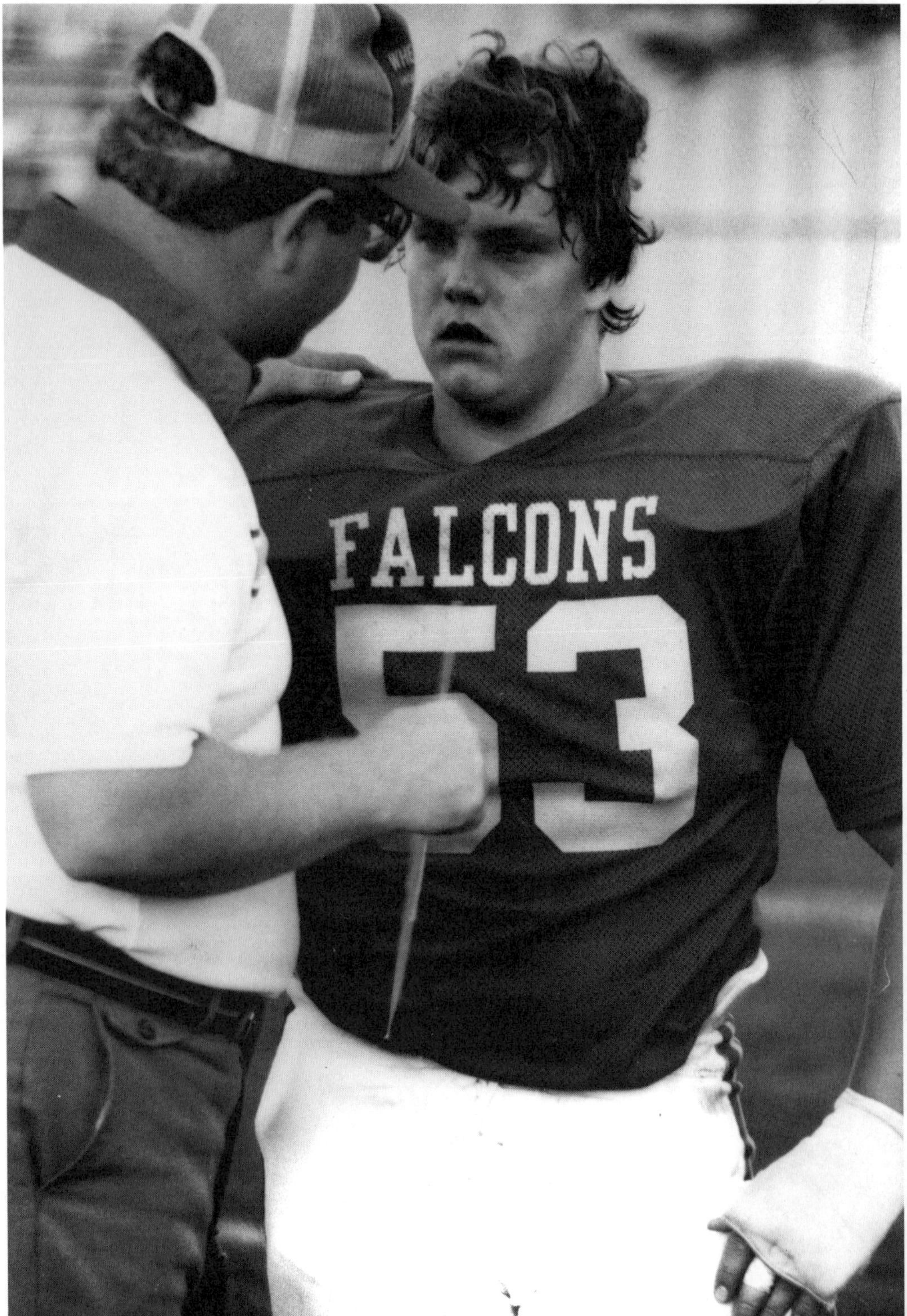
FALCONS
53

SESSION 3

Injuries and Doubts

CROWD BREAKER

See *Coach's Book.*

ONVERSATION STARTER

Groups of 2 / 15 minutes

You Are What You Eat. To get started, get together with one other person from your team (not the same person as in the last session) and share your eating habits. Take the first half-finished sentence and let both partners finish the sentence. Then, take the second sentence and both share, etc. If you have time left over, answer the two questions about your partner's habits under FEEDBACK.

1. My favorite food is ...

2. My favorite place to eat out is ...

3. My favorite dessert is ...

4. I draw the line when it comes to eating ...

5. If I could eat anyplace in the world, I would choose ...

6. My idea of a midnight snack is ...

7. On a first date, I would probably eat at ...

8. If this was a really special person, I might take this person to ...

9. If I could order something "way out," I might order ...

10. My favorite meal in the year with my family is ...

11. The most bizarre thing I ever ate was ...

12. The food that best describes my personality in the morning is ...

Feedback: Answer these two questions about your partner.

1. If you could take your partner out to eat, where would you choose to go?

2. Who does your partner remind you of in their personality?

Groups of 4 / 15–30 minutes

 Seeing Is Believing. Sooner or later, every Christian will have spiritual struggles and doubts—when you feel like your prayers go no higher than the ceiling. Someone you love dies unexpectedly and you wonder if God is asleep at the switch. You are disappointed in a relationship—and you wonder if God cares.

This is what this session is all about—spiritual struggles and doubts. The story in the Bible that you will look at is the story of Thomas—often called "Doubting Thomas." For some reason, he was not in the room after the Resurrection when Jesus appeared to the disciples. And he refused to believe them when they said Jesus was alive.

Listen to the story. Then, move into groups of 4 and discuss the questionnaire: (1) **Looking Into the Story**—about the Bible story, and (2) **My Own Story**—about your own experience. Remember, there are no right or wrong answers, so feel free to speak up.

Be sure to save the last 20 minutes at the close to get back together with your team of 8 and debrief the session.

²⁴Now Thomas (called Didymus), one of the Twelve, was not with the disciples when Jesus came. ²⁵So the other disciples told him, "We have seen the Lord!"

But he said to them, "Unless I see the nail marks in his hands and put my finger where the nails were, and put my hand into his side, I will not believe it."

²⁶A week later his disciples were in the house again, and Thomas was with them. Though the doors were locked, Jesus came and stood among them and said, "Peace be with you!" ²⁷Then he said to Thomas, "Put your finger here; see my hands. Reach out your hand and put it into my side. Stop doubting and believe."

²⁸Thomas said to him, "My Lord and my God!"

²⁹Then Jesus told him, "Because you have seen me, you have believed; blessed are those who have not seen and yet have believed."

John 20:24–29

Looking Into the Story: In groups of 4, let one person answer question #1, the next person answer question #2 ... etc. around your group.

1. Who does Thomas remind you of in this story?
   - ▣ a science teacher
   - ❑ an agnostic
   - ❑ an honest person who wanted to believe
   - ❑ a friend of mine
   - ❑ myself
   - ❑ other:_____

2. "Unless I see the nail marks in his hands and put my finger where the nails were, and put my hand into his side, I will not believe it." What is Thomas saying here?
   - ❒ You guys are crazy!
   - ▣ I need proof.
   - ❒ Don't put me on.
   - ❒ I really want to believe you, but ...
   - ❒ other:_____

3. How did Jesus deal with Thomas' doubts?
   - ❒ He bawled him out for his unbelief.
   - ▣ He gave him the evidence he asked for.
   - ❒ He gave him another chance.
   - ❒ He challenged Thomas to accept him on faith.

4. What would be your prediction for how Thomas' faith was *after* this story?
   - ❒ He probably never learned to get past his doubts.
   - ❒ He learned his lesson, and believed from this point on.
   - ▣ Voicing his doubts helped him have a stronger faith than others who never admitted such things.
   - ❒ He forever felt guilty for doubting, and this hurt his witness.

My Own Story: Note the change in sharing procedure. Let everyone share their answer on each question. Remember to save the last 20 minutes at the close for Caring Time.

1. What is the closest that you have come to going through what Thomas went through?
   - ❒ when my parents got divorced
   - ❒ when someone close to me died
   - ❒ when I stopped going to church
   - ❒ when I tried really hard but failed
   - ❒ when I was disappointed and took it out on God
   - ❒ other:_____

2. What do you rely upon for spiritual "proof"?
   - ❒ gut feelings/instinct
   - ❒ what the Bible says
   - ❒ what my church teaches
   - ❒ logic/common sense
   - ❒ emotional peace
   - ❒ Christian friends
   - ❒ simple faith
   - ❒ other:_____

3. If you could ask God one "hard question" about your spiritual life, what would it be?
    ❏ How do I deal with doubt?
    ❏ How do I deal with guilt?
    ❏ What's wrong when I don't always *feel* like a Christian?
    ❏ Where is God when I'm hurting?
    ❏ Why can't I seem to get closer to Jesus?
    ❏ other:_____

4. When you have spiritual doubts, what does that indicate?
    ❏ My faith is weak.
    ❏ I need some more information.
    ❏ I need a spiritual "checkup."
    ❏ Growth may be taking place.
    ❏ other:_____

5. When you have struggles and doubts in your faith, what have you found helpful?
    ❏ going to the Bible
    ❏ talking it over with my youth leader
    ❏ sharing my struggles with my friends
    ❏ letting my friends share their struggles
    ❏ going to church/youth group
    ❏ going ahead "on faith"
    ❏ other:_____

6. When you feel really down and you have to talk to someone about your spiritual struggles and doubts, who do you go to?
    ❏ my mom/dad
    ❏ my best friend
    ❏ my youth leader/pastor
    ❏ a special teacher/coach
    ❏ nobody
    ❏ other:_____

7. How do you feel talking about these things right now?
    ❏ funny
    ❏ okay, but ...
    ❏ fine
    ❏ uncomfortable
    ❏ I wish we did this more often in our youth group.
    ❏ other:_____

Groups of 8 / 15–20 minutes

How Do You Feel About Your Team? You have been with your team now for three sessions. Take your pulse on how you feel about your group. Steps 1 and 2 are for your team together. Step 3 is with your prayer partner.

Step 1: Report In. If you could compare your involvement in this program to the diagram below, where would you be?

- In the grandstand—for spectators—just looking on
- On the bench—on the team—but not playing
- On the playing field—where the action is
- In the showers—on the injury list

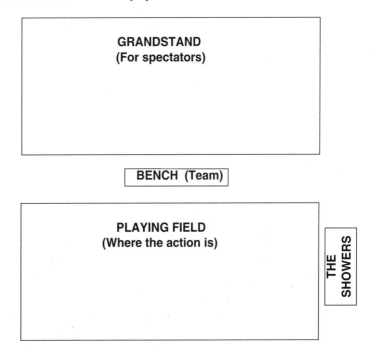

Step 2: Teamwork. How would you describe the way you work together as a team?

- We're playing more like individuals than like a team.
- We're just starting to trust each other.
- Our teamwork is awkward—but improving.
- We're on a roll—like a championship team.

Step 3: Prayer Partner. Get together with your prayer partner and check to see how last week went. Then, spend a little time in prayer for each other. Start off by picking a number from 1 to 10—1 being TERRIBLE and 10 being GREAT—to describe how last week went.

SESSION 4
Equipped for Battle

See *Coach's Book.*

Groups of 2 / 15 minutes

Quiz Show. This session is the mid-point in this course. Be sure to set aside time at the close to make a halftime report.

In this session, you will be dealing with the battle in the Christian life. To get started, get together with one other person from your team. In silence, circle one answer for each of the seven questions below. Then read the first question out loud and let your partner try to guess your answer. Say your answer and let your partner jot down in the margin the money they won if they guessed right. Read the next question and let your partner guess again, etc. until you have gone through the list.

Then it's your partner's turn ... with you guessing their answers. At the end, the person with the most money WINS.

For $1, I am more likely to take a:
a. shower   b. bath

For $2, when eating chicken, I choose:
a. drumstick
b. breast
c. wings

For $3, if a movie gets scary, I:
a. go to the bathroom
b. close my eyes
c. clutch a friend
d. love it

For $4, in buying clothes, I look for:
a. fashion/style
b. quality
c. price
d. name brand

For $5, in movies, I prefer:
a. comedy
b. action/adventure
c. science fiction
d. horror film
e. Disney animation
f. serious drama

For $6, when I undress at night, I put my clothes:
a. on a hanger in the closet
b. folded neatly over a chair
c. stuffed into the hamper
d. tossed in the corner
e. left on the floor

For $7, to relax, I prefer:
a. being alone
b. being in a crowd
c. being with a few friends

Groups of 4 / 15–30 minutes

 Armed for Battle. Nobody promised that the Christian life was going to be easy. Jesus called it the narrow gate. In the Scripture for this session, the apostle Paul calls the Christian life a fight and he goes on to compare the equipment of the Christian to a Roman soldier fully dressed for battle.

The questionnaire for this Bible study is going to be a little different. In the first half, you will be taking a test on yourself. In the second half, you will reflect on your life and check out some Scripture for answers.

Now move into groups of 4 and listen to the Scripture passage. Then, discuss the questionnaire below. There are no right or wrong answers, so feel free to express your opinions. Be sure to save the last 20 minutes at the close to regather with your team and evaluate the first half of this course.

[10]Finally, be strong in the Lord and in his mighty power. [11]Put on the full armor of God so that you can take your stand against the devil's schemes. [12]For our struggle is not against flesh and blood, but against the rulers, against the authorities, against the powers of this dark world and against the spiritual forces of evil in the heavenly realms. [13]Therefore put on the full armor of God, so that when the day of evil comes, you may be able to stand your ground, and after you have done everything, to stand. [14]Stand firm then, with the belt of truth buckled around your waist, with the breastplate of righteousness in place, [15]and with your feet fitted with the readiness that comes from the gospel of peace. [16]In addition to all this, take up the shield of faith, with which you can extinguish all the flaming arrows of the evil one. [17]Take the helmet of salvation and the sword of the Spirit, which is the word of God. [18]And pray in the Spirit on all occasions with all kinds of prayers and requests. With this in mind, be alert and always keep on praying for all the saints.

Ephesians 6:10–18

Looking Into the Story: In groups of 4, let one person read the first piece of equipment below and the application of this equipment. Then, go around your group and let everyone call out a number from 1 to 10—1 being VERY LOW and 10 being VERY HIGH. And explain why you gave yourself this number.

Then, read the next piece of equipment and application and let everyone call out another number, etc. through the list.

Belt of truth

I am prepared to stake my life on the fact that Jesus Christ is the Son of God. I have thought through what I believe, and I am willing to take a stand.

| 1 | 2 | 3 | 4 | 5 | 6 | 7 | 8 | 9 | 10 |

Breastplate of righteousness

I am prepared to put my life where my mouth is—in clean and right living—with genuine integrity—as Christ did. I am serious about being God's man/woman.

1   2   3   4   5   6   7   8   9   10

Feet fitted with the readiness that comes from the gospel of peace

I am willing to publicly affirm my faith in Christ—at school, work or wherever. I find it easy to talk about my personal faith.

1   2   3   4   5   6   7   8   9   10

Shield of faith

I am prepared to step out with Christ—to risk my life, my fortune and my future to him whatever the cost or consequences. And through faith, I am taking a stand against the "evil one."

1   2   3   4   5   6   7   8   9   10

Helmet of salvation

I know that I am part of the family of God because of Jesus Christ. I have a strong inner peace because I am at peace with God.

1   2   3   4   5   6   7   8   9   10

Sword of the Spirit, which is the word of God

I actively seek to know more about God and his will for my life through an ongoing study of his guidebook, the Bible. I discipline myself to reflect on it daily.

1   2   3   4   5   6   7   8   9   10

Prayer

I set aside time regularly to talk with God and to let him speak to me. I consciously try to submit every decision in my life to God.

1   2   3   4   5   6   7   8   9   10

Personal Reflection:

Go around on these two questions and let everyone explain their answer.

1. After taking this test on yourself, how do you feel right now?
    - ❐ terrible   ❐ challenged
    - ❐ encouraged   ❐ embarrassed
    - ❐ exposed   ❐ other:_____

2. If you could pick one promise for your life right now, what would you choose? Read over the Scripture verses below and explain to the group which verse you would like to take home with you for this coming week.

I can do everything through him who gives me strength.
Philippians 4:13

Therefore, if anyone is in Christ, he is a new creation; the old has gone, the new has come!
2 Corinthians 5:17

Do not conform any longer to the pattern of this world, but be transformed by the renewing of your mind. Then you will be able to test and approve what God's will is—his good, pleasing and perfect will.
Romans 12:2

Consider it pure joy, my brothers, whenever you face trials of many kinds, because you know that the testing of your faith develops perseverance.
James 1:2–3

"Ask and it will be given to you; seek and you will find; knock and the door will be opened to you. For everyone who asks receives; he who seeks finds; and to him who knocks, the door will be opened."
Matthew 7:7–8

For through the law I died to the law so that I might live for God. I have been crucified with Christ and I no longer live, but Christ lives in me. The life I live in the body, I live by faith in the Son of God, who loved me and gave himself for me.
Galatians 2:19–20

And we know that in all things God works for the good of those who love him, who have been called according to his purpose.
Romans 8:28

... being confident of this, that he who began a good work in you will carry it on to completion until the day of Christ Jesus.
Philippians 1:6

"Come to me, all you who are weary and burdened, and I will give you rest. Take my yoke upon you and learn from me, for I am gentle and humble in heart, and you will find rest for your souls. For my yoke is easy and my burden is light."
Matthew 11:28–30

"Here I am! I stand at the door and knock. If anyone hears my voice and opens the door, I will come in and eat with him, and he with me."
Revelation 3:20

Groups of 8 / 15–20 minutes

 Mid-Course Affirmation. It's halftime. Time for a break. Get together with your team of 8 (or the whole group if you have 12 or less) and evaluate your experience so far.

Here are two options. The second option is more risky, but a lot more personal if you are comfortable with it.

Option 1: Halftime Progress Report. Turn to the Progress Report on page 3 and let everyone report any growth in their lives since being in this program.

Option 2: Appreciation Time. Ask one person on your team to sit in silence while the others share one thing that they have come to appreciate about this person. Finish one of these sentences:

Since being in your group, I have come to see you as ...

or

Since being in your group, I have come to appreciate you for your ...

After you have gone around your group on the first person, ask the next person to sit in silence while the others finish the sentence on this person ... etc. around the group.

This is called "strength bombardment" or "appreciation bombardment." You've done a lot of talking about yourself during this program. Now you will have a chance to hear what the others on your team have learned about you. Get set for a beautiful experience in AFFIRMATION.

If you don't know how to get started, look over the list below and pick out a word or two words that help describe what you see in this person ... and tell them so.

I SEE YOU AS VERY ...

loyal	nice	warm	crazy
peaceful	cheerful	dedicated	courageous
dependable	loving	gentle	special
daring	cool	kind	thoughtful
fun	sensitive	compassionate	energetic
open	prayerful	perceptive	encouraging
generous	spiritual	strong	beautiful
lovable	caring	sincere	persistent
friendly	together	playful	confident

SESSION 5
Heavy Stuff

CROWD BREAKER

See *Coach's Book*.

Groups of 2 / 15 minutes

CONVERSATION STARTER

Last Day on Earth. This starts the second half of this course. Up to now, you have talked about your spiritual life in general. Now, you will have a chance to deal with some of the deeper issues you will have to face.

To prepare for the Bible study later, get together with one other person from your team and discuss this question,

If you had only one more day to live, what would you do?

In silence, read over the list and check (✔) the items that you would want to do for sure. Then, break the silence and share what you checked with your partner.

IF I HAD ONLY ONE MORE DAY TO LIVE, I WOULD ...

____ Perform some high-risk feat that I have always wanted to do, figuring that if I don't make it, it won't really matter.

____ Stage an incredible robbery for a large amount of money which I would immediately give to the needy and starving of the world.

____ Not tell anyone.

____ Use my dilemma to share Christ with as many people as I could.

____ Make my own funeral arrangements.

____ Spend a great deal of time in prayer and Bible study.

____ Offer myself to science or medicine to be used for experiments that might have fatal results.

✓ Spend my last day with my family or close personal friends.

____ Write a diary about my life (or my last day).

____ Try to accomplish as many worthwhile projects as possible.

____ Have as much fun as possible (sex, parties, booze, whatever turns me on).

29

Groups of 4 / 15–30 minutes

Down ... but Not Out! There comes a time in the life of every Christian when you have to decide who is going to sit on the throne of your life—you or God.

Interestingly, Jesus had to face this very decision. He faced it just before he was arrested and taken away to be crucified. He was in a garden—praying. He knew that Judas had gone to get the temple police to arrest him. Jesus still had time to run away and avoid all the pain. But he had to decide. Immediately.

Jesus took his three closest friends with him to this garden to pray. Listen to the story. Then, move into groups of 4 and discuss the questionnaire. Be sure to save the last 20 minutes in the session to get back together with your team and debrief what you learned.

[36]Then Jesus went with his disciples to a place called Gethsemane, and he said to them, "Sit here while I go over there and pray." [37]He took Peter and the two sons of Zebedee along with him, and he began to be sorrowful and troubled. [38]Then he said to them, "My soul is overwhelmed with sorrow to the point of death. Stay here and keep watch with me."

[39]Going a little farther, he fell with his face to the ground and prayed, "My Father, if it is possible, may this cup be taken from me. Yet not as I will, but as you will."

[40]Then he returned to his disciples and found them sleeping, "Could you men not keep watch with me for one hour?" he asked Peter. [41]"Watch and pray so that you will not fall into temptation. The spirit is willing, but the body is weak."

[42]He went away a second time and prayed, "My Father, if it is not possible for this cup to be taken away unless I drink it, may your will be done."

[43]When he came back, he again found them sleeping, because their eyes were heavy. [44]So he left them and went away once more and prayed the third time, saying the same thing.

[45]Then he returned to the disciples and said to them, "Are you still sleeping and resting? Look, the hour is near, and the Son of Man is betrayed into the hands of sinners. [46]Rise, let us go! Here comes my betrayer!"

Matthew 26:36–46

Looking Into the Story: In groups of 4, let one person answer question #1, the next person question #2, etc. around the group.

1. Why do you think Jesus went to the garden to pray?
    - ❒ That's what religious people are supposed to do.
    - ❒ He prayed at the same time every day and it was time.
    - ☑ He was stressed out and needed strength and guidance.
    - ❒ He wanted to give a good example to his disciples.
    - ❒ It was his last chance to ask God for a plan other than the cross.

2. Why did Jesus take three friends with him?
   - ❐ He needed companionship.
   - ❐ He wanted an eyewitness to record this event.
   - ❐ He wanted these guys to see the pain that he had to go through.
   - ❐ He needed protection.
   - ❐ He wanted them to pray for him.

3. If Jesus knew that his mission was to go to the cross, why was he flinching at doing God's will?
   - ❐ He knew that the cross was painful.
   - ❐ Being human, he was scared.
   - ❐ He had the same battle that we all face—doing God's will.
   - ❐ The closer he got to the cross, the worse the pressure became.
   - ❐ He dreaded taking the sins of the world upon himself.

4. Why did the three closest friends that Jesus had on earth fall asleep when he needed them most?
   - ❐ They were tired.
   - ❐ They didn't know what he was going through.
   - ❐ They had too much to eat at the Last Supper.
   - ❐ That's the way friends are at times.

My Own Story: Note the change in the instructions for discussion. Let everyone share their answer for each question.

1. Where is the "Garden of Gethsemane" that you go to when you have to make big decisions?
   - ❐ my bedroom
   - ❐ my favorite place outdoors
   - ❐ church
   - ❐ the ball park
   - ❐ family vacation home
   - ❐ I don't really have a place.
   - ❐ other:_____

2. If you were facing a big, big decision and you wanted three friends to be with you, whom would you ask?
   - ❐ someone in my youth group
   - ❐ some of my classmates
   - ❐ my best friend and my parents
   - ❐ I'm not sure I have three friends, maybe one.
   - ❐ I don't know of anybody.

3. If these three friends fell asleep on you, what would you do?
   - ❏ pour cold water on them
   - ❏ let them sleep
   - ❏ feel sorry for them
   - ❏ cry
   - ❏ yell at them
   - ❏ understand

4. In your lifetime—from birth to right now—what is the closest you have come to this kind of Gethsemane experience: "God ... not what I want, but what you want." Put a mark somewhere on the line to indicate this experience in your life.

   BIRTH_____**RIGHT NOW**

5. What is the biggest issue you are facing in your spiritual life?
   - ❏ sorting out my values
   - ❏ choosing the right friends
   - ❏ making time for God every day
   - ❏ cleaning up my life
   - ❏ breaking some old habits
   - ❏ dealing with my sexual desires
   - ❏ knowing what God wants me to do with my life
   - ❏ other:_____

6. What is harder for you?
   - ❏ knowing what God wants me to do
   - ❏ doing what I know God wants me to do
   - ❏ standing alone when my friends don't support me
   - ❏ being consistent

7. How would your parent(s) react if you told them some of the issues you have to deal with?
   - ❏ They would be shocked.
   - ❏ They might kick me out of the house.
   - ❏ I don't know, I never talk to them.
   - ❏ They would listen and understand.
   - ❏ other:_____

8. How would your youth group react if you told them about some of these issues in your life?
   - ❏ I don't talk about the heavy stuff at youth group.
   - ❏ They would understand.
   - ❏ We deal with stuff like this all the time.
   - ❏ I'm not sure.
   - ❏ other:_____

9. When it comes to doing the will of God, how would you finish this sentence? "I desire to do God's will ..."
   - ❏ all of the time
   - ❏ most of the time
   - ❏ some of the time
   - ❏ occasionally

Groups of 8 / 15–20 minutes

 Getting Personal. Here are two options to choose from to close this session.

Option 1: Follow the usual procedure. Regather as teams and report in on the session—what you learned—and spend some time in prayer with your prayer partner.

Option 2: Try a new form of sharing prayer requests and praying for one another. If you choose this option, here are the instructions.

1. Get together in groups of three. (Some groups may need to have four persons.)

2. Let one person share a prayer request by answering the question:

   How can we help you in prayer this week?

3. The other two respond to this prayer request in this way:

   • One person prays a prayer of *thanks* ...

   "God, I want to thank you for (name) ..."

   • The other person prays a prayer of *petition* ...

   "God, I ask your help for my friend (name), for ..."

4. When you have finished with the first person, let the next person share a request and the other two pray for this person, etc. ... around the group of three.

   Remember, in your group of three, you start out by letting one person answer this question.

   "How can we help you in prayer this week?"

Rainy Days

CROWD BREAKER

See *Coach's Book.*

Groups of 2 / 15 minutes

CONVERSATION STARTER

 A Fantasy Date. You are almost finished with this course. Next session will be the last. Are you planning a party or some way to celebrate this experience?

In this session, you will be dealing with the issue of consistency—or inconsistency—in your Christian life. To get started in this session, get together with one other person from your team and have each of you create a fantasy date with a famous person. Use the questions below. When one of you have finished, reverse the roles and let the other person talk.

LEADER: We recommend that you divide the group into guys and girls for this session.

CONGRATULATIONS! You just won the National Dating Contest.

1. If you could have a date with any famous person—movie star, athlete, music artist, etc.—who would it be?

2. Where would you like to go on this date—any place in the world—sporting event, concert, restaurant, outdoor activity, etc.?

3. How would you get there—plane, limousine, boat, carriage?

4. How would you want to dress? And how about your date?

5. What about a special gift for this occasion—flowers, jewelry, perfume/cologne, CD?

6. How about some music for this occasion? What would you like?

7. Surprise. A very, very famous person is on the phone to say hello and wish you well. Who would you like this person to be?

8. Suddenly, over the loud speaker, there is an announcement. Your favorite song is going to be played in honor of you and your date. What would you like for them to play?

Groups of 4 / 15–30 minutes

Charting Your Spiritual Life. Everybody is entitled to a "rookie" year. In the rookie year, you expect inconsistency—goofs, mistakes, poor judgment, bloopers. Even the greatest quarterbacks had a rookie year. In this Bible study, you will have a chance to trace Simon Peter's rookie year and see how he went through a lot of ups and downs spiritually. In fact, you are going to trace his ups and downs on a chart.

You may want to stay together as a whole group and let your youth leader lead you through the first part of this exercise. Then, move into groups of 4 to share your own story.

Looking Into the Story: The following are seven episodes from Peter's life with Christ (remember, we saw in Session 1 that Jesus called Peter "Cephas" or "the rock"). For each experience, try to pinpoint how he felt and put a dot on the graph—somewhere between 1 and 10—1 being THE PITS and 10 being GREAT.

For instance, for the first episode you might pinpoint his feelings at 9—because you think he was thrilled to be invited to be on Jesus' team. When you have finished with all seven episodes, connect the dots to get a picture of Peter's spiritual ups and downs.

A. Jesus' Call to Peter: *As Jesus walked beside the Sea of Galilee, he saw Simon and his brother Andrew casting a net into the lake, for they were fishermen. "Come, follow me," Jesus said, "and I will make you fishers of men." At once they left their nets and followed him.* Mark 1:16–18

B. Jesus Heals Peter's Mother-in-Law: *Simon's mother-in-law was in bed with a fever, and they told Jesus about her. So he went to her, took her hand and helped her up. The fever left her and she began to wait on them.* Mark 1:30–31

C. Peter's Confession of Christ: *"But what about you?" he asked. "Who do you say I am?" Simon Peter answered, "You are the Christ, the Son of the living God." Jesus replied, "Blessed are you, Simon son of Jonah, for this was not revealed to you by man, but by my Father in heaven."* Matthew 16:15–17

D. Peter Rebukes Jesus: *From that time on Jesus began to explain to his disciples that he must go to Jerusalem and suffer many things at the hands of the elders, chief priests and teachers of the law, and that he must be killed and on the third day be raised to life. Peter took him aside and began to rebuke him. "Never, Lord!" he said. "This shall never happen to you!" Jesus turned and said to Peter, "Get behind me, Satan! You are a stumbling block to me; you do not have in mind the things of God, but the things of men."* Matthew 16:21–23

E. Peter Falls Asleep: *They went to a place called Gethsemane, and Jesus said to his disciples, "Sit here while I pray." He took Peter, James and John along with him, and he began to be deeply distressed and troubled. ...Then he returned to his disciples and found them sleeping. "Simon," he said to Peter, "are you asleep? Could you not keep watch for one hour? Watch and pray so that you will not fall into temptation. The spirit is willing, but the body is weak."* Mark 14:32–33,37–38

F. Peter Denies Christ: *While Peter was below in the courtyard, one of the servant girls of the high priest came by. When she saw Peter warming himself, she looked closely at him. "You also were with that Nazarene, Jesus," she said. But he denied it. "I don't know or understand what you're talking about," he said, and went out into the entryway. When the servant girl saw him there, she said again to those standing around, "This fellow is one of them." Again he denied it. After a little while, those standing near said to Peter, "Surely you are one of them, for you are a Galilean." He began to call down curses on himself, and he swore to them, "I don't know this man you're talking about." Immediately the rooster crowed the second time. Then Peter remembered the word Jesus had spoken to him: "Before the rooster crows twice you will disown me three times." And he broke down and wept.* Mark 14:66–72

G. Peter Sees the Tomb: *So Peter and the other disciple started for the tomb. ... Then Simon Peter, who was behind him, arrived and went into the tomb. He saw the strips of linen lying there, as well as the burial cloth that had been around Jesus' head. The cloth was folded up by itself, separate from the linen.* John 20:3,6–7

Sample:

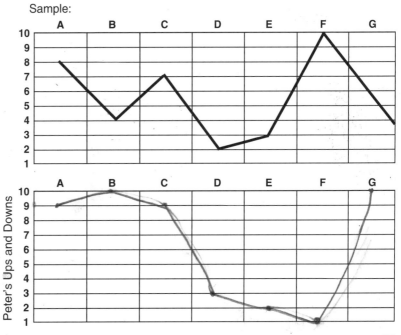

37

My Own Story: Note the change in the sharing instructions. In groups of 4, let everyone answer each question.

1. If you pinpointed the high point in your spiritual experience ... or the time in your life when you felt spiritually high, what would it be?

2. As you think back, what made you feel spiritually high at that time?

3. If you pinpointed the low point in your spiritual experience ... or the time in your life when you felt spiritually low, what would it be?

4. What made you feel spiritually low at that time?

5. Now, with the two points that you have already established, could you create a graph to show the ups and downs in your spiritual life like the one you did for Peter? (Hint: you may want to divide your life into years, or 2-year or 3-year spans.)

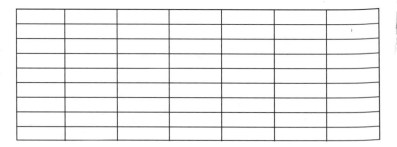

6. What insight do you learn from this exercise?
   - ❏ that God had a plan for my life—even when I felt low
   - ❏ that God uses the painful experiences to build character
   - ❏ that God works in spite of us sometimes
   - ❏ that God isn't through with me yet
   - ❏ that in all things God works for the good of those who love him

Groups of 8 / 15–20 minutes

Learning to Care. You are nearly through with this course as a youth group. Next week, you will have a chance to celebrate and decide what you are going to do next. To prepare for your last session together, take a few minutes right now and reflect on how you have changed during this course.

1. **Affirmation.** Go around and let everyone on your team answer one or more of the questions below. If you know each other fairly well, you can use this time to share how you have seen your team-mates grow.

   • Where have you grown in your own life during this course?
   • Where have you seen growth in some of the others in your group during this course?
   • What have you liked most about the group during this course?

2. **Options.** At this point, your team can choose one of two ways to close the meeting.

   • **Option 1: Prayer Partners.** Get together with your prayer partner and report on your week. Then close in prayer.

   • **Option 2: Circle of Love.** Stay together with your team and express your feelings for each other non-verbally. Here is how. Follow carefully:

   a. Stand in a circle—about a foot apart.

   b. Everyone puts their right hand in front of them—palm up.

   c. Team Leader steps into the circle and goes to one person, looking them in the eyes for a few seconds. The leader then takes that person's hand and tries to express the care he or she feels for this person by doing something to their hand—such as gripping it firmly, stroking it, shaking it ... etc. Use only appropriate gestures.

   d. After the Team Leader has gone around the circle, the next person goes around the circle in the same way, etc. ... until everyone has gone around the circle.

   Remember, all of this is done *without words.*

   In shaking the hands of those in your group, you can say a lot— like how you care!

SESSION 7
Way to Go

CROWD BREAKER

See *Coach's Book*.

PREPARATION FOR CLOSING

Individual Exercise / 5 minutes

Animal Affirmation. Instead of the usual Conversation Starter, we suggest that you devote five minutes right now to prepare for the Caring Time at the close of this session.

In silence, read over the list of animals below as you think about the members of your team. If you had to pick an animal that reminds you of their personalities, which animals would you pick—a different animal for each person on your team.

Do NOT tell anyone what you have picked. Just make your selections now and wait until later to share.

_____ PLAYFUL PORPOISE: intelligent, lively, the life of the party

_____ CUDDLY TEDDY BEAR: lovable, warm, brings out the "mother" in all of us

_____ PUPPY DOG: fun-loving, irresistible, disarming, childlike

_____ MOTHER HEN: caring, sensitive, always on the lookout for the well being of others

_____ WILD EAGLE: untamed, noble, independent, cherishes freedom and the wide-open spaces

_____ FAITHFUL SHEEP DOG: loyal, dependable, devoted, always there when you need someone

_____ HUNGRY CHEETAH: quiet, unassuming, sleek, on the prowl and usually gets their prey

_____ WISE OLD OWL: quiet, thoughtful, with the appearance of being in deep contemplation

_____ GRACEFUL SWAN: majestic, smooth-sailing, unruffled—always in command of the situation

_____ PEACEFUL DOVE: calm, behind-the-scenes peacemaker in the midst of storms

_____ COLORFUL PEACOCK: fun, outrageous, flashy

_____ TIRELESS TURTLE: slow and steady, persistent plodder—but willing to stick their neck out at times

_____ HONEY BEE: energetic, tireless worker

Groups of 4 / 15–20 minutes

The Last Word. If you were going to leave your friends for good, what would be the last thing you would want to tell them?

The Scripture for this session is the final words that Jesus shared with his disciples. It is fitting that we study these words—known as the Great Commission— in the final session in this course. Keep in mind the setting. The 11 disciples are back in Galilee. Jesus asked them to gather at this mountain. Listen to the story. Then, move into groups of 4 and discuss the questionnaire.

Be sure to save 30 minutes at the close to regather the entire youth group and evaluate your experience in this course. Now, move into groups of 4 and listen to Jesus' last words to his disciples.

¹⁶Then the eleven disciples went to Galilee, to the mountain where Jesus had told them to go. ¹⁷When they saw him, they worshiped him; but some doubted. ¹⁸Then Jesus came to them and said, "All authority in heaven and on earth has been given to me. ¹⁹Therefore go and make disciples of all nations, baptizing them in the name of the Father and of the Son and of the Holy Spirit, ²⁰and teaching them to obey everything I have commanded you. And surely I am with you always, to the very end of the age."

Matthew 28:16–20

Looking Into the Story: In groups of 4, let one person answer question #1, the next person answer question #2, etc. around the group.

1. Jesus has just risen from the dead, and gives these instructions to his disciples prior to ascending to heaven. What does his speech at this point most remind you of?
    - ❐ a football coach giving a "win one for the Gipper" speech
    - ❐ the president talking to the nation about his legislative agenda
    - ❐ my parents telling me what to do just before leaving me in charge of my younger brother/sister
    - ◼ a counselor giving me advice about my future

2. Had you been one of the disciples at this time, what information that Jesus gave them would have been most important to you?
    - ◼ that he had authority over everything in heaven and on earth
    - ❐ that he wanted me to help by spreading the word
    - ❐ that he would be with me at all times
    - ❐ that a time would come when history would come to a close

3. How ready were the disciples to carry on his work when Jesus commanded them to, "Go and make disciples of all nations"?
    - ❐ totally unprepared
    - ❐ They knew a little bit.
    - ❐ They had each other.
    - ◼ If they weren't ready, Jesus wouldn't have sent them out.

4. If you were a betting person, would you bet on these 11 disciples carrying out the Great Commission?
   ☐ absolutely not
   ☐ Well, I'd give them a 10% chance.
   ☐ maybe 50/50
   ☒ Sure, because they had the Holy Spirit.

My Own Story: Note how the instructions for sharing shift. Everyone answers each question. Remember to save the last 30 minutes at the close for the evaluation/Caring Time.

1. If you were to compare your Christian life right now to a football game, where would you be?
   ☐ waiting for the game to start   ☒ suiting up
   ☐ sitting on the bench   ☐ playing "catch up"
   ☐ at halftime—resting   ☐ tuckered out
   ☐ on the injury list   ☐ giving it all I've got

2. What is your favorite way of dodging issues of Christian disciple-ship—like not sharing the Good News of Christ?
   ☐ claiming I don't understand
   ☐ saying I don't have time
   ☐ acting too cool to care
   ☐ thinking others can do it
   ☒ putting things off
   ☐ other:_____

3. What have you learned since being in this course that might help you in sharing your faith?
   ☐ that it is not "sissy" to be a Christian
   ☐ that you don't have to be "perfect" to be a Christian
   ☒ that others struggle with the same stuff that I struggle with
   ☐ that the Christian life is exciting
   ☐ that Jesus is the Son of God
   ☐ that God gives everyone a "second chance"
   ☐ other:_____

4. If you could pay a compliment to your youth group for helping you in your spiritual life, what would you want to thank them for?
   ☐ being with me and letting me talk about my problems
   ☐ forcing me to check out my values on some things
   ☐ sharing some of their own problems
   ☐ helping me deal with some of my relationships
   ☐ giving me encouragement
   ☐ other:_____

5. If you had to go in for a spiritual checkup right now, how would you do? On the following scale, circle a number from 1 to 10—1 being VERY LOW and 10 being VERY HIGH in each category. Then, get together and read one category and let all four call out their number. Then, read the next category and let everyone call out their number, etc. through the list.

In living out my commitment to Christ:
1   2   3   4   (5)   6   7   8   9   10

In reshaping my lifestyle around spiritual values:
1   2   (3)   4   5   6   7   8   9   10

In working for justice for all peoples:
1   2   3   4   5   (6)   7   8   9   10

In thinking of my long-range goals:
1   2   3   4   5   (6)   7   8   9   10

In experiencing God's inner peace:
1   2   3   4   5   6   (7)   8   9   10

In discovering my own special gifts:
(1)   2   3   4   5   6   7   8   9   10

In putting my money where my mouth is:
1   (2)   3   4   5   6   7   8   9   10

In developing a daily devotional habit:
(1)   2   3   4   5   6   7   8   9   10

In keeping my thoughts under God's control:
1   (2)   3   4   5   6   7   8   9   10

In standing up for what I believe:
1   (2)   3   4   5   6   7   8   9   10

In controlling my temper:
1   2   (3)   4   5   6   7   8   9   10

In dealing with family relationships:
1   (2)   3   4   5   6   7   8   9   10

In managing my time for best use:
(1)   2   3   4   5   6   7   8   9   10

In sharing my faith with my friends:
(1)   2   3   4   5   6   7   8   9   10

Groups of 8 or All Together / 25–30 minutes

What Happened? You have two options for this special closing experience: (1) A debriefing session, using the agenda below, or (2) The worship service as described in the *Coach's Book*, Session 7, for the book *Beginnings*.

LEADER:
Decide whether to use the steps here or the worship service in the *Coach's Book* (or a combination of the two). If you use the steps here you will also need to decide whether to break into the teams of 8 or all stay together.

1. **Affirmation:** Regather as teams (or the entire youth group together) and share the results of the exercise you did on your own at the start of the meeting. Ask one person to sit in silence while everyone on their team explains what they chose for this person and why. Then, move to the next person, etc. around the group. Use this opportunity to share your appreciation for the contributions you have made to each other on the team.

2. **Evaluation:** Go around on each question below and let everyone explain their answer.

    A. When you first started this course, what did you think about it?
    - ❏ I had some reservations.　❏ I liked it.
    - ❏ I only came for the fun.　❏ I was bored.
    - ❏ other:_____

    B. How would you describe the experience of opening up and sharing your ideas and problems with this group?
    - ❏ scary
    - ❏ very difficult
    - ❏ exciting
    - ❏ a life-changing experience
    - ❏ invaluable
    - ❏ okay, but ...
    - ❏ just what I needed
    - ❏ a beautiful breakthrough

    C. What was the high point in this program for you?
    - ❏ fun
    - ❏ finding myself again
    - ❏ times of prayer
    - ❏ Bible study
    - ❏ knowing I am not alone in my problems
    - ❏ feeling of belonging to others who really care
    - ❏ being with teammates who are committed to Christ
    - ❏ learning to deal with my hang-ups

3. **Personal Change:** Turn back to page 3 and let everyone share one area in which they have changed during this course.

4. **What's Next?** As a group, discuss what you are going to do next. You might decide to do another study. Or perhaps plan a group service project or retreat. There are two youth series with nine books in each series available from Serendipity, plus the 12 Group Bible Study books for youth/adults. For more information contact Serendipity at 1-800-525-9563.

A Word to the Youth Leaders

Congratulations. You are working with the most potential-packed audience in the world—teenagers. This is one of the most difficult times in their lives. They are making big decisions, often alone or in packs. Peers are important to them and there is tremendous pressure to do what peers demand. This youth program is designed to give teenagers a feeling of belonging. A family of peers. An alternative to the gang at school or the gangs on the streets. Maybe even an alternative inside of the school.

This program is built around the idea of teamwork. The goal is to help youth "bring out the best in one another." By agreeing on a set of goals. By agreeing on a level of commitment for a period of time (seven weeks). By setting ground rules and holding each other accountable. If this sounds like something out of educational psychology, it is. The dynamics are the same. The only difference is the motive and the learning objective. The goal of this program is spiritual formation. Christian orientation. Christian value clarification. Christian moral development. Christian commitment.

The Importance of Voluntary Commitment

The difference between this program and the typical youth program in the church is the commitment level. To get into this program, a youth *must* commit himself or herself to being in the program. This means "choosing" to be in the program every session for seven weeks, to be a team player in order to make the group process work.

Anyone who has been involved in team sports will understand this principle. And anyone who has coached a team will understand the role of the youth leader. The youth leader is the coach and the youth group is the squad. The squad is broken up into small units or teams of six to eight—with an assistant coach or facilitator inside of each team.

Structure of the Youth Meetings

The meetings look like typical training workouts of a sports camp. First, the whole squad meets together for some optional limbering up exercises called Crowd Breakers (all together or by teams of 8 if you have a large youth group). Then, the entire squad pairs off for some basic, one-on-one Conversation Starters to break the ice. Then, with these partners, groups of 4 are formed for the Bible Study discussion. Finally, the team of 8 is regathered for a wrap-up and Caring Time for each other. The typical meeting looks like this:

Step 1:	Step 2:	Step 3:	Step 4:
Crowd Breaker /	Conversation	Bible Study /	Wrap Up and
Teams of 8	Starter /	Groups of 4	Caring Time /
or all together	Groups of 2	or half of team	Teams of 8

Moving from the large group (Step 1) to groups of 2 (Step 2) to groups of 4 (Step 3) to groups of 8 (Step 4) will not only offer a spontaneity to the meeting, but will also position the youth to be in the best size group for the particular type of activity.

Step 1:	**Step 2:**	**Step 3:**	**Step 4:**
Purpose: To kick off the meeting	Purpose: To build relationships	Purpose: To discuss Scripture	Purpose: To care for one another

In the first session in this course, the ideal would be to form teams of 8 that can stay together for the entire course. This could be done by random selection or by designating the teams to break up cliques. Or it can be done in a serendipitous fashion by giving out slips of song titles and having the youth find out who is on their team by whistling their song until they "find each other." For junior highs, we recommend that an adult or older youth be in each team of 8.

If you have more than 12 youth, we recommend dividing into teams of 6 to 8 for Step 1 and Step 4. If your group is not more than 12, you may want to keep everyone together for Step 1 and Step 4. At any rate, break into groups of 2 for Step 2 and groups of 4 for Step 3. (If you have less than six youth, you may prefer to stay together for the entire meeting.)

In Case of Emergency, Read the Instructions

In the margin beside each Step, you will find instructions to the leader. Be sure to read them. Sometimes the instructions are very important. Trust us. We have written this program based on our experience. Give the program a chance. There is a method to the madness—particularly the fast-paced movement from 2s to 4s to 8s.

We also recommend using the *Coach's Book* that accompanies this series and is available separately. It includes a game plan and a choice of two Crowd Breakers for every session.

Get a commitment from your youth before you start the program for seven weeks or seven sessions. And remind them of it (by thanking them every week for making this commitment). Here's to what God is about to do in your youth. Here's to the future of your church—your youth.

Serendipity House is a publisher specializing in small groups. Serendipity has been providing training and resources for youth ministry for over 30 years. As we continue to develop materials for youth groups, we would love to hear your comments, ideas or suggestions. Call us at 1-800-525-9563.

SERENDIPITY HOUSE

SERENDIPITY HOUSE is a publishing house that creates programs like this one for many types of groups in the church: kickoff groups, Bible study groups, support groups, recovery groups and mission/task groups. The philosophy behind these groups is the same: (1) help the group agree upon their purpose and ground rules, (2) spend the first few sessions together getting acquainted, (3) shift gears in Bible study as the group matures, and (4) help the group say "goodbye" and decompress when they are through with their purpose.

ABOUT THE AUTHOR

LYMAN COLEMAN has been a pioneer of the small group movement since the 1950s. During this time he has trained thousands of youth leaders and pastors in the conversation Bible study method through Serendipity seminars. The uniqueness of this series of Bible studies is the group approach to Scripture study—where group building is central in the sharing and caring for one another in a youth group.

Lyman is indebted to the thousands of youth leaders over the years who have helped in the development of the Serendipity youth ministry model. Lyman is especially grateful to Denny Rydberg (President of Young Life), co-author of the first edition of this material, and the Serendipity staff who have worked on this third edition—Matthew Lockhart, Andrew Sloan, Sharon Penington and Erika Tiepel.